Tobie Edward Parsons

John Albert Monroe, a memorial:

Recollections of him as commander of Battery D

Tobie Edward Parsons

John Albert Monroe, a memorial:
Recollections of him as commander of Battery D

ISBN/EAN: 9783337815295

Printed in Europe, USA, Canada, Australia, Japan

Cover: Foto ©ninafisch / pixelio.de

More available books at **www.hansebooks.com**

PERSONAL NARRATIVES

OF EVENTS IN THE

WAR OF THE REBELLION,

BEING PAPERS READ BEFORE THE

RHODE ISLAND SOLDIERS AND SAILORS

HISTORICAL SOCIETY.

FOURTH SERIES – No. 18.

PROVIDENCE:

PUBLISHED BY THE SOCIETY.

1892.

John Albert Monroe

A Memorial.

RECOLLECTIONS OF HIM AS COMMANDER OF

Battery D:

By GEORGE C. SUMNER.

A Biographical Sketch:

By GEORGE B. PECK, M. D.

A Eulogy:

By EDWARD P. TOBIE.

PROVIDENCE:

PUBLISHED BY THE SOCIETY.

1892.

Recollections of J. Albert Monroe,

As Commander of Battery D, First Rhode Island Light Artillery.

By George C. Sumner, Formerly of Battery D.

My early recollections of Colonel Monroe are so interwoven with those of Battery D, that any reminiscences which I might indulge in of the one, would, necessarily, include the other.

My acquaintance with him began on the 15th of September, 1861, on the occasion of his becoming connected with Battery D as its first commander, and were continued through that important part of his military career, during which he made for himself that grand record as an organizer, instructor and intelligent disciplinarian of light artillery. A record which soon brought him promotion, first to

major, then lieutenant-colonel of our regiment, and
drew the attention of the projectors of the Artillery
Camp of Instruction at Washington to the extent of
his being chosen to organize and command that camp,
where he equipped and drilled to efficiency many batteries, earning the proud distinction of having had
the third largest command of light artillery in the
war, being exceeded only by Generals Barry and
Hunt.

When we consider that our friend received this
appointment from an officer of the regular army, a
West Point graduate, having presumably all the
prejudices against and lack of faith in volunteer
officers, known to have been entertained by many
" West Point graduates " in those early days of the
war, and that he had as an opponent for the position
an officer who possessed that qualification, we can
imagine how much Colonel Monroe's record had
impressed the appointing power with his ability and
fitness to fill the position.

When Colonel Monroe first looked upon Battery
D he saw an assemblage of about one hundred and
fifty boys—not one in ten of them had reached his

majority—most of them from good homes, where they had received fair educational advantages, unused to restraint, certainly the restraint of a proper military discipline; filled with a spirit of independence and love of freedom to be expected in boys whose forefathers had written that wonderful declaration for freedom's sake, and totally unaware of what it would be necessary for them to pass through in the way of irksome discipline and tedious drill before they could become serviceable soldiers.

Hard lessons were to be learned, that all wills must be subordinated to one will, which must be supreme and obeyed, right or wrong; an unswerving devotion to duty, implicit confidence in their officers, and the greatest possible efficiency in drill must be acquired. These lessons were to be taught them by a young man in the twenty-fifth year of his age, having the full knowledge that he had almost absolute control over their bodies, and so far as any outward expression was concerned, of their minds. I speak of this, Mr. President, because with my thirty years of added experience with human nature, it seems to me most marvelous that it was accom-

plished with so little friction, for I do not remember
a single instance of serious insubordination during
his stay with us, which convinces me that it was
done with moderation and intelligence.

I well remember that during this will-subduing
period there would occasionally be one encountered,
which would require all of the powerful helps at the
command of the captain, such as an indefinite residence at the guard-house on a diet of bread and
water, the spare wheel, backing a log, etc., before
it could be brought into even seeming subjection.
That there was grumbling and growling among
the boys you may be sure. Could you have heard
the discussions of their trials and tribulations when
they were quite sure they would not be overheard,
you would very likely have been led to believe that
the captain had been guilty of some very oppressive
and arbitrary acts, but I am certain that a careful
analysis of these claims would have proven them to
amount in importance to the single case of reprimand
which I remember to have received from him. I
had been called to his tent to explain why I had performed a certain duty in a way different from which

he had ordered. I began by saying that I thought so and so. He stopped me, and in his most imperious manner demanded to know what right I had to think, and informed me that he was employed and paid by the government to do my thinking for me. I remember that I construed this language literally, and it so distressed the young American eagle within me, that nothing but fear of the consequences prevented it from screaming with rage. That I, a young man of intelligence (please remember that this was a seventeen year old estimate of intelligence), was to be debarred the privilege of thinking for myself, seemed to me to be the very worst of debasement. My views upon the enormity of his offence have changed wonderfully in the years that I have lived since those days; for I have seen many times when I could have wished that he was still employed to do my thinking.

I believe that Colonel Monroe always tried to discriminate between harmless and vicious infraction of discipline. I remember instances when just for fun escapades were indulged in that would have necessitated his punishing the participants had he felt that they knew that he was familiar with their frolic ; but although he was considered almost omnipresent, they felt sure that he knew nothing about this or that particular case. In conversation with me recently, he has astonished me with his familiarity with many such cases.

It has seemed to me as I have meditated upon those old days in recent years, that Colonel Monroe had made up his mind from the beginning that there were great possibilities for this battery ; that he had perhaps said to himself, here is a personnel from which, by persistent hard labor in drill and a proper application of disciplining, there can be evolved a battery of light artillery which will be an honor to their state and themselves. Certain am I that the persistent hard labor was indulged in, beginning with the very first days of his connection with us ; it was continued without interruption through the fall, winter and spring, even upon the march (when in the early spring we had made an advance toward Centreville), if the army turned aside for a day's rest, Battery D would be taken out for a field drill, and, if the weather happened to be against that, the manual of the piece would be indulged in.

Sunday was our only day of rest, but even then we were obliged to spend nearly the whole forenoon at inspection, either mounted or on foot. Now this constant work had by the time of our arrival in front of Fredericksburg, on April 19, 1862, made itself apparent in the increased ease and accuracy with which the movements were made. Colonel Monroe was not satisfied that the movement was executed; it must be done perfectly—perfection must be aimed at. Every detail received his attention. He appeared to think, and endeavored to convey the impression to us, that he believed if a right or left wheel could be made with the pivot gun at a walk, and a perfect alignment maintained, that it was just as possible to make the same movement equally successfully with the pivot gun at a trot. He seemed to have no patience with the men, if, after a half hour's close interval drill back and forth over the same ground, too many tracks were visible, and if a stranger could have heard his condemnatory remarks on such occasions, they would immediately have concluded that he considered us the worst lot of blockheads in the world; but he did not; on the contrary, he was proud of us. How many times I have seen him as he moved us out of park, down past the Lacy House, opposite Fredericksburg, where he knew there would be more or less of an audience, composed of major-generals, brigadier-generals and officers of lesser rank, together with prominent civilians from all over the north, occasionally from our own state, and seen that smile of satisfaction as he whirled us over those extensive level fields in that most exciting manœuvre, a field drill, his whole manner indicating that should his thoughts be expressed in words they would be, " Just look at us, did you ever see it done better ? "

Now I well remember that this constant drill did not meet with the entire approbation of the men ; they could not see the necessity of such long-continued and persistent work. Their anger exhibited itself in broken poles and harnesses, acts which gained for the perpetrator the privilege of standing on the head of a barrel or backing a log, until he was sorry he had not done the best he could at drill, and controlled his anger.

What the men of Battery D needed was a severe

practical illustration of the necessity and importance of all this exacting discipline, and, as they considered it, excessive drill. The time was fast approaching when they were to receive just such a lesson, which was to be so thoroughly and intensely practical in its teachings that it would settle forever in their minds the supreme importance of these preparatory measures and the correctness of their captain's judgment. Perhaps in no way could I convey to you what I consider to be evidence most positive of the success of Colonel Monroe's rigorous training, both in its discipline which had so firmly fixed in the mind of every man, that the first and most important duty of a soldier was prompt obedience to orders under all circumstances, for in no other way could that unity of action be maintained which would make the service of the battery efficient and effective, and the drill with which they had been so thoroughly familiarized, even to its minutest detail, that the execution of the various manœuvres had become almost as much of an instinctive act as walking, as by a description of the action of the men in this their first battle.

2

About 4 o'clock on the afternoon of the 30th of August, 1862, Battery D found itself in position on the crest of a hill overlooking a tract of country which a little more than a year before had been the scene of a great disaster to our army. As it was then, so it began to be apparent to the men of our battery as we stood watching the conflict while waiting for the time to come when we should take part, it was to be again, for away off on the right we could plainly see our troops being overwhelmed by the enemy and driven back. That our time of trial was fast approaching is made evident by a cloud of dust, which like a snake has been crawling along, until now it has reached our front, and we are earnestly watching for the appearance of the enemy that we may open upon them. Soon we notice a cloud of dust and considerable commotion upon a hill something more than a mile away; the dust has hardly settled when we see a puff of smoke, and in a few seconds a case-shot explodes in our midst. Captain Monroe orders that we commence firing, and our struggle has commenced.

At the foot of the hill upon which we are, there

runs a brook, the water in which is very low, and a thin line of blue has taken position along the farther bank, constituting what was expected to be our support. Soon this line open fire upon the enemy, who are approaching through the woods ; the rebels reply to their fire and the struggle is continued for a few moments, when the enemy charges, our line of blue breaks, rushes up the hill through our intervals to the rear. Our support has failed, and Battery D is face to face with the enemy, who rush en masse out of the woods, jumping into the depression of the brook, where they tarry long enough to correct their formation. There is not a doubt in the mind of a single one of those rebels but that this lone battery is to be taken, for cannot they see that success is attending the efforts of their comrades? (at this very moment one of our batteries is being captured by them, not more than half a mile to the right and front of our position). All these things which are so encouraging to them are just as discouraging to us. It is evident to every man of us that we shall have to leave our position or become prisoners. But Captain Monroe has determined that he will not leave until he has tested the ability and valor of his men to the fullest. The rebels have perfected their formation and started for the battery; already they have covered nearly half the distance, and it looks bad for us, but listen! did you ever hear more rapid firing? Certainly guns were never served faster than these. Let us watch the cannoneers for a moment. The gun has just been discharged; each cannoneer has been watching the muzzle of his piece, and the moment he saw the flash he jumped for and seized the wheels of the gun carriage, thereby saving half the recoil. Instantly No. 3 jumps for his position and covers the vent with his left thumb, protected by a thumb-cot. Clear and cool-headed must he be, for if that vent be not well covered while No. 1 (who reached his position at the same moment with No. 3) is sponging the piece, a spark of fire may be left which will cause a premature explosion. No. 1 has finished sponging, and while he has been reversing his sponge-staff, No. 2 inserted a double round of canister, which No. 1 sends home with a long swinging motion of his body, and in a instant you hear the warning from the gunner " Ready ;"

Nos. 1, 2 and 3 assume that position, No. 4 inserts his primer, and the command " Fire ! " is heard immediately.

It has taken less than thirty seconds to do this; yes, three times in a minute will this movement be repeated. The gun is getting hot; you can hardly bear your hand upon it; No. 3's thumb-cot is gradually being burnt through to the flesh. His captain has told him that should that occur it would be his duty to hold on with his bare thumb though the flesh be burnt to the bone, and he will do it. The hands and faces of Nos. 1 and 2 have become blackened with powder-soot; more than once have they been obliged to change places because of the exhausting labor of No. 1. Did you notice that while the piece was being loaded the gunner was at work with the elevating-screw, raising the breech and lowering the muzzle of the gun? If you had looked across that gun you would have said that that charge would certainly be wasted, for it was being thrown into the ground; but if you had watched the effect of the discharge, you noticed that it struck the ground a few yards in front of the enemy, and that its rebound reached them at just the right height to do the most damage.

Such rapid and effective firing as had met this assault was more than the enemy could stand, and they fell back.

While the battery has been thus engaged, the enemy has placed other batteries in position, and they are now filling the air with bursting shells, while canister goes ricochetting through the battery with fearful frequency. Did ever so much danger lurk in so small a space? Now the enemy has started for us again, with the evident determination that there shall be no failure on their part to possess our battery. Their attack is more upon our flanks than front. The direction of our right and left pieces is changed and we are doing them much damage, when it is reported to the gunner that our canister is all gone, and that only a few rounds of solid shot remain. We cannot cover much ground with this kind of ammunition. The enemy discover this almost as soon as we, there is no infantry to oppose them, and anywhere outside of the direct range of our pieces is as safe ground for them as though they were miles away.

Quickly taking advantage of this, they seek those places, and make for us as fast as possible. "If these guns are saved they will have to be limbered immediately. I doubt there being time even now," said General Milroy. But our captain has his own ideas about that, and his men are content to wait for his order. A moment later and it is given, "Limber to the rear." The limbers are whirled across the trail of the pieces, which are instantly limbered and are whirled away, almost from the actual possession of the enemy.

Right here occurred the most convincing evidence, to my mind, of the thoroughness with which every detail of the drill had been impressed upon the minds of those men. Among the details of Captain Monroe's instructions was one regarding the care of the implements of the piece, such as sponge-staff, water-bucket, handspikes, etc., which under no circumstances were to be forgotten and left upon the field, for the loss of them might disable the piece and render it useless; and now as we are leaving this field, with the enemy in hot pursuit, it suddenly flashes through the mind of a gunner that he has left the handspike of his piece; a cannoneer remembers that a water-bucket has been left, for which he is responsible, and at the risk of their lives these men rush back, secure the articles, and, wonderful to relate, reach their battery in safety

We now move to the rear battery front at a smart trot for several hundred yards, when we are almost made speechless with astonishment by the order, " To the rear in battery!" What did it mean? Could it be possible that Captain Monroe did not know of our lack of ammunition, or does he desire to see if the men will yield prompt obedience to an order which he knows full well is absurd? If this be his object, the result must have been very satisfactory, for before the last notes of the bugle had died away, every gun had been unlimbered, the limbers were whirled into position and the cannoneers were at their posts. After a few moments we again limbered and moved off the field.

Colonel Monroe has been pleased to say, in a paper read before this Society, that after this day's experience with the men of Battery D, he should not have hesitated to march through the whole Confederacy with them. I can say for the men of Battery D, that after this day's experience with their captain they would, had he desired it, been perfectly willing to have followed him on just such a trip.

Much had been accomplished by this day's work; a mutual confidence had been established which promised well for future service, but alas for Battery D, they had learned to appreciate their captain just as they were about to lose him. His ability had been seen by others, and he was wanted for a larger work. Only once more was he to take them into battle, and the gallant and successful manner in which he led us down through that dreadful corn-field at Antietam, placed us in that very unusual and hazardous position, accomplished promptly and satisfactorily the difficult task demanded of him by General Hooker, bringing off all of his pieces save one, which was afterwards rescued by volunteers from his own company, will ever remain in the minds of the men of Battery D.

On the 21st of October he was promoted to major, and left the battery. The genius of Colonel Monroe, his great executive ability, the intelligence of his judgment, as evidenced by the remarkable success which attended his labors while in command of Battery D, gained for him the unqualified admiration and esteem of his men. He had none of that element in human nature known as personal magnetism. His dignity of manner, which prevented all familiarity, and the sharp and decided character of his speech, which left no opportunity for argument or reply, prevented the men from warming into that enthusiasm for him which would have been the case if his nature had been different.

It was many years after Colonel Monroe left Battery D before I saw him again. Occasionally within recent years I have seen him at the meetings of this Society, and my respect for, interest in, and admiration of the man led me to desire as intimate and close personal intercourse with him as possible ; but when the opportunity came and I made the attempt, I saw in his manner what I imagined to be indifference, which cooled my ardor and prevented my continuing the effort.

But I had not touched the right chord. There came a time when there entered my heart a desire such as has entered yours, Mr. President, and the heart of every old soldier in this room, to meet once again the men in whose companionship I had passed through the most trying epoch of my life. Men who had participated in the same trials and troubles, had shared the same dangers, endured the same suffering and distress; who during that terrible winter of '64 in East Tennessee, when in an almost starved and half-frozen condition for weeks at a time, with no prospect of having my necessities in either direction relieved, and life had not seemed worth the living, had from a condition no better than my own, by word or deed extended to me that sympathetic comradeship which encouraged me to make the effort necessary to keep life within me. And the desire grew and grew until I could resist it no longer, and with the assistance of my old comrade and friend, Captain Gray, a reunion was arranged. An invitation was sent to Colonel Monroe, but I confess I had no thought that there was sentiment enough in his heart towards us for a favorable response; and you may judge of my surprise at receiving a letter from him thanking me for the invitation, expressing great

regard for the men of Battery D, and declaring that
nothing but sickness or death would prevent his being present on that occasion. He was present, and
it was the unanimous desire of the fifty-five members of his old battery that he should serve them as
president. That was a great day for us, Mr. President. Our hearts were full to overflowing. In the
language of an old comrade, " It was easy to laugh,
and it was just as easy to cry," either expressed the
same sentiment.

To no one did the day bring greater pleasure than
to our commander. I caught an occasional glimpse
of his heart on that day, but on the morning of the
next, when I reached my office, I found him waiting
for me, and the enthusiasm of his greeting, the evident depth of feeling with which he expressed his
thanks for the day's pleasure, which he was pleased
to say I had given him, and his expressions of love
and admiration for my comrades of Battery D was a
revelation to me. It was as though that exterior
which had always seemed to me so repellant and un-
approachable, had suddenly been thrown off, as one
would a cloak, and left exposed to my view a heart
filled with love, pathos and sentiment.

That this interview warmed my heart towards my old commander you may be sure. During the remainder of his life—about eleven months—he honored me with much of his society, which would have been very pleasant but for the fact that in the enjoyment of it I was obliged to witness the steady progress of, and intense suffering from, the malignant growth which was so soon to end his life.

I feel that I have very imperfectly conveyed to you my full estimate of Colonel Monroe; there is much more that I should like to say of him did time permit, but I shall have to content myself in closing by saying that the record of Col. John Albert Monroe is one which not only brought honor to himself, but also to his state, and of which his fellow citizens may justly feel proud. Of him it may be truly said, that, having the ability, he used it to its fullness in the service of his country

3

John Albert Monroe: A Sketch.

[*From the Adjutant's Report of the P. M. C. A. Veteran Association, presented May 11, 1892.*]

Geo. B. Peck, Jr., Late Lieutenant Second Regiment Rhode Island Volunteers and more recently Major Providence Marine Corps of Artillery.

John Albert Monroe, the model artillerist, a representative citizen soldier and an illustrious example of the value of the militia as a war school, is with us no longer. He was born in Swansea Village, Mass., Oct. 25, 1836, of John Sheldon and Louisa Hunter Monroe. He is the fourth lineal descendant of Thomas Monroe, who in 1652 came to this country from England with two brothers, John and James. A grandson of the latter obtained considerable reputation subsequently as the fifth president of the United States. John Albert attended the public schools of Fall River until the age of thirteen, when stern necessity, which makes heroes of striplings and giants of common folk, drove him from home, thenceforth to wage the battle of life single-handed. He first found employment in a dry goods store in Boston, where he remained more than two years. An insatiable thirst for knowledge *for its own sake*, which characterized his entire life, early manifested itself, for in 1852 he entered the Providence High School, his parents having changed their residence for a second time and to this city His carefully hoarded savings permitted, however, but little more than two years of study. A favorable opportunity for replenishing his purse presented itself in the jewelry manufactory of his uncle, William Monroe, with whom he labored two years steadily, and afterward upon occasion. A winter's experience at Fruit Hill as a teacher was not without influence in moulding and developing his character, but attendance upon the East Greenwich Academy and the University Grammar School furnished the excellent preparatory training that promised the highest rank in his college class. He entered Brown in 1860 with the intention of pursuing a four years' course, but his eyes were so inflamed from over-study that he felt constrained to forego the further pursuit of Greek letters, and hence would have graduated in 1863. Most of his associations and his strongest sympathies were, however, with the members of the class of 1864. Upon its re-unions he was a frequent attendant; from its members he received always most cordial and fraternal welcomes. Naturally this occurred, for had not all alike and together experienced the vicissitudes of that most miserable set of unfortunates, Freshmen? As such I first met him on the college campus. The then exceeding disparity of our years occurred not to me, and I remained a stranger thereto until his demise. There seemed, however, a certain strength and stability of character behind or rather sustaining a frank, kind, though upon occasion somewhat brusque manner that riveted my attention and secured a regard that has simply been intensified by the developments of three decades. At this time he was strengthening his exchequer by serving as librarian to the Franklin Lyceum, for half a century the most popular and influential literary and debating society in this city.

Of Monroe's college mates those of '63 attained their greatest success on the tented field. Generals William Ames and Charles R. Brayton, of the Third Rhode Island Heavy Artillery, with Col. William W Bliss, of the Eighty-seventh United States Colored Troops, most nearly approached him in their records. The class of '64 is obliged to rest content with civic honors won by President Seth J Axtell, of the Central University of Iowa, Judge George M. Carpenter, of the United States District Court, and Hon. Oscar Lapham, of the National House of Representatives.

Monroe enrolled himself as an active member of the Marine Artillery Sept. 22, 1854, and his first period of service corresponds presumably with his artizan life. He was chosen fourth corporal in April, 1856, but acted as fifth sergeant during the excursion to Woonsocket in October of that year. The ensuing spring he was regularly elected to the latter position, but resigned May 11th. His name was placed on the fined list.

When the war broke out Monroe was anxious to enter the field with the First Battery He refrained only upon intimation by Governor Sprague that he had other work for him. No sooner had Captain, more recently General, Charles H. Tompkins sailed with his command than these doors were thrown wide open for the organization of the Second Battery, afterwards known as Battery A, to which he was appointed drill-master. He entered upon his new duties with alacrity, taking unusual pains to instil into the new recruits that true military spirit essential to soldierly success. How thoroughly this was accomplished is shown not only in the battery's brilliant history, but in the records of Brevet Lt.-Col. T. Fred Brown, Captains George E. Randolph and Charles D. Owen, Lieuts. G. Lyman Dwight and Charles H. Clarke, all of the First Regiment Rhode Island Light Artillery, and Brevet Major Harry C. Cushing, now of Battery B, but formerly of Battery H, Fourth United States Artillery, all of whom were non-commissioned officers of that battery at this time, and received their first instruction in the art of war from him. The manner of his teaching is sufficiently evinced by the presentation on June 6, 1861, the date of his commission as second lieutenant

(according to the popular nomenclature of the time,
but absolutely junior first lieutenant) of the Second
Battery, of an elegant sabre by the enlisted men,
through the late Hon. Cæsar A. Updike. He afterwards received a first lieutenant's commission bear-
ing the same date, was made captain of Battery D,
Sept. 7, 1861; major, Oct. 21, 1862, and lieutenant-
colonel, Dec. 4, 1862. He was mustered out of service Oct. 5, 1864.

Time would fail to give in detail Monroe's service
record. Is it not already a part and an important
part of Rhode Island history? And of United States
history as well? An outline of the staff duty performed and a list of the engagements participated in
must suffice. He was chief of artillery to the divis-
ions of McDowell, Doubleday and Hooker success-
ively; commander of the Artillery Camp of Instruction at Washington, D. C.; chief of artillery
commanding the artillery brigade of the Second
Army Corps; inspector and chief of staff of the artillery reserve of the Army of the Potomac; commanding officer of the second division of the artillery brigade of the Eighth Army Corps, and chief of

artillery commanding the artillery brigade of the Ninth Army Corps. When instructing artillerymen (both officers and privates) in their duties, he frequently formed line with twenty batteries, occasionally with twenty-eight, though seldom undertaking to manœuvre more than the former number at one time, thus exercising a larger independent direct artillery command than has ever been accorded to any officer in any army of the United States save Generals Hunt and Barry, both West Point graduates. He also particularly distinguished himself by the promptness, accuracy and effectiveness of the fire of all his batteries at the explosion of the mine before Petersburg, July 30, 1864. Had all the details of Burnside's arrangements similarly escaped the miserable tamperings of the contemptibly jealous George G. Meade, the history of the last days of the Rebellion would have been far different and much briefer.

Monroe's battle record is as follows : Fairfax Court House, First Bull Run, Falmouth ; Tar, Po and North Anna rivers ; (cavalry skirmish), Thoroughfare Gap, Rappahannock Station, Sulphur Springs, Gainesville, Groveton, Second Bull Run, Annan-

dale, South Mountain, Antietam, Kelly's Ford,
Mine Run, Locust Grove, Morton's Ford, Tolopot-
omy, Bethesda Church, Hawes' Shop, Cold Harbor,
Wilderness, Po River, Spottsylvania, North Anna,
First Assault of Petersburg, Fort Hell, Siege of Pe-
tersburg, Mine Explosion, Avery Farm, Yellow
Tavern and Pegram's Farm.

At the very height of the war, July 1, 1863, Colonel Monroe married a most estimable young lady,
Miss Mary Catherine Bodkin, daughter of Washington Lee Bodkin, of Alexandria, Va. Although her
father died some years before the war, so pronounced
were the secession sentiments of other and distant
relatives that government withheld a brigadier's
commission that had already been filled out lest the
national interests should in some manner be com-
promised, a significant commentary on the doubt
and suspicion then prevailing as to the loyalty of
some officers much higher in authority. His affec-
tion, however, was something more than fancy or
sentiment: ephemeral rank weighed little against
life's happiness. The intensity of his devotion was
still more clearly manifested during the closing

weeks of the long years in which she resolutely and
heroically fought that fell destroyer, consumption,
when he relinquished all professional engagements
that he might the more perfectly minister to her com-
fort and happiness; not less clearly in subsequent
fidelity to her memory. Three daughters survive
their parents' deaths, Mary Albert, wife of J. Frank
McBride, of Newburg, N. Y., Blanche Annette and
Josephine Amelia.

When the colonel had adjusted his final accounts
with the war department, he returned to this city

The bread and butter question is paramount for a
gentleman with family, and accordingly he embraced
the first promising opportunity for securing those
necessities by conducting a newspaper and periodical
depot on the ground floor of the Roger Williams
Hotel building on North Main Street, first door above
the What Cheer Building. Here I renewed my
antebellum acquaintance and sought that wisdom a
raw recruit naturally desires on entering the field
beside war-worn veterans. Although I had anxiously
asked many men presumably capable of giving ad-
vice, he was the only one who could impart definite

information as to the proper contents of an officer's valise and the articles desirable to have at hand on the march. This incident, trifling in itself, clearly indicated his thorough knowledge of and careful attention to seemingly insignificant details. I also incidentally discovered that the entire volume of artillery tactics was at his tongue's end, also the Army Regulations save certain tables and forms that could not by any possibility be useful to him.

Early in June, 1866, Monroe entered the office of Cushing & DeWitt, civil engineers, at No. 21 South Main Street, and commenced his real life work, which was pursued with unremitting zeal and energy almost to the hour of death. The trials and the triumphs of the quarter century cannot be compressed within the limits of this sketch. Only those monuments most noticeable to the popular eye can be designated. He superintended the construction of the railroad bridge at India Point in 1867, and at the mouth of the Connecticut River in 1868. He designed and built the Rondout viaduct, also the Thames river railroad bridge, which occupied his time for the two years preceding Oct. 11, 1889. The water works system of Bismarck, Dakota, and the sewer system of Mt. Desert, Maine, are scarcely less conspicuous, while his survey of the Mississippi from Cairo to Memphis is possessed of even greater practical importance.

Colonel Monroe became an active participant in the affairs of the Marine Artillery for a second time at the annual election of 1867 During the war we of the home guard were compelled to admit to its ranks, in order that required duties might properly be performed, a very undesirable element of the population, a set of men that were very good food for powder, but too destitute of "sand" to perform the best acts to them possible. Two or more, barely capable of performing properly a sergeant's duties, had been given commissions in 1866, and now the gang loudly boasted they would capture the entire organization. The friends of the battery rallied, and after a determined contest, elected Maj. Joseph P Balch, who commanded Burnside's regiment at Bull Run and the Marine Artillery on its excursion to Boston in 1852, when it was the only battery of "flying artillery" in the United States outside the regular army to the charge of its interests. For duty sergeants under me as first sergeant were chosen Brevet Brig.-Gen. John G Hazard, Lieut. Frank A. Rhodes, Capt. Edwin C. Gallup, Capt. Jeffrey Hazard, Lieut.-Col. J. Albert Monroe, and (militia) Col. Frank G. Allen. I owed my position to the simple fact that I was acquainted with the men and knew from whom we should free ourselves. My *subordinates* (?) took hold with a will and faithfully performed all duties required of them in the armory, dropping out only as the process of re-organization progressed. The Fourth of July, however, came upon us long before much had been accomplished. Yet salutes must be fired. The Marines must parade. We did the best we could. One section, now termed platoon, appeared in the procession under the command of Lieut. Gilbert H. Hagan. I took charge of the right piece, but John Albert Monroe was the only man who would consider for an instant taking charge of the left. He paraded that day wearing an old coat that had been handed down from Sprague's administration, with plain service chevrons on his sleeves, a forage cap on his head,

4

and a regulation cavalry sabre by his side. His
shoulders were ornamented with a tarnished pair of
scales. The day was intensely hot. I never more
narrowly escaped sunstroke. Covered with dust
and severely burned, we looked charmingly! No
stranger would ever have dreamed that chap had
commanded thousands! Yet he simply noted certain duty *must* be performed, and as there was none
other to discharge it, he assumed it with the same
imperturbable manner that characterized him on
more conspicuous occasions under infinitely greater
responsibilities. This simple incident is of the
highest importance as an index of the man's character, revealing in a single act the depth of his modesty, his fidelity and his loyalty Fortunate that
man, that institution, that country, that cause, that
can count such an one a friend!

Reorganization being well nigh effected, Monroe
was chosen unanimously lieutenant-colonel commanding by the active corps in 1868, and again in 1869, but
professional engagements calling him from home, he
resigned his charge on the 7th of June. Once again
he accepted a commission—that of captain—in 1880,

another emergency having occurred that seemed to require the influence of his personal presence to insure the corps a safe passage by all dangers. He was made an honorary member upon the acceptance of his resignation, and elected engineer on the honorary staff, which position he filled save when on active duty as above indicated until 1884. His name stands third on the signature book of this association. He served as our quartermaster from 1876 to to 1882 inclusive, also in 1884.

Although Colonel Monroe was every inch a soldier and every inch a mechanician, there is another element of his constitution markedly noticeable, the more because ordinarily alien to if not inconsistent with such proclivities and such pursuits, and that is an unusual fondness for literature and an aptitude for literary work. Not only did he make important contributions to the American Society of Civil Engineers, of which he was a senior member at the time of his death, and to the papers of the Rhode Island Soldiers and Sailors Historical Society, which he assisted in founding, and of whose publication committee he was for years an important member,

but the letters, reports and general articles that have
appeared not only in the *Journal* and other local
papers but also in those published where from time
to time he has bivouacked, are well nigh innumera-
ble. His style was clear, chaste and vivacious, without attempt at display, and exhibited a general
scholarship hardly to be expected in one so thoroughly identified with the sternest and most practical
occupations of life. It was known to him as well as
to others that had his days been prolonged but another
week he would have received from that university,
whose full benefits he would gladly have enjoyed,
and in whose welfare he was ever interested, that
recognition to which his eminent services and thorough attainments long since entitled him.

If one should ask what single act in Monroe's life
best and most completely illustrates the man and
his powers, I should unhesitatingly reply his hand-
ling of Battery D at the Second Bull Run. Passing
with briefest allusion the perfection of drill and implicit mutual confidence indicated by its withdrawal
intact from the very crest of a wave that almost
completely engulfed every other battery in line, the

sublime audacity or the grim humor which suggested
the *idea* of checking once and again, even for a few
moments, the advance of the swarming rebel hordes
with his half dozen twelve-pounders, unsupported
and alone, seems well nigh inconceivable. No feat
of the artillery arm that has come to my knowledge,
not even Stewart's celebrated charge at Bethesda
Church, which is not without its counterparts, has
ever equaled it. The more I consider it the more am
I awe-stricken at its magnitude. Equally impres-
sive was his steadfast regard for his old commander,
William Sprague. While many who humbly bowed
to the famous war governor hardly recognized him
in the hour of his adversity, Monroe remembered
his obligations not only as an individual but as a citizen, and freely accorded at all times and at all places
that appreciation and regard due from every member
of this commonwealth.

Colonel Monroe died suddenly from hemorrhage
resulting from cancer of the jaw, just after noon, on
Thursday, June 11, 1891, at the age of fifty-four
years, seven months and sixteen days. His remains
were interred at Grace Church cemetery. They were

followed to the grave by the Veteran Association of Battery D, the Veteran Association of the First Regiment Rhode Island Light Artillery, by Department Commander Benjamin H. Child and staff of the Grand Army of the Republic, with which order the colonel early identified himself, and by Rodman Post, No. 12, G. A. R., of which he was commander in 1878–9, all being under the escort of Battery A, Brigade Rhode Island Militia, which is the old Marine Artillery, performing duty in conformance to the state law and army regulations.

COLONEL J. ALBERT MONROE,

(Died June 11, 1891.)

BY EDWARD P. TOBIE

———◆———

COLONEL MONROE is dead. We saw him reverently laid at rest, and turned away with tears—tears of joy for him that he had escaped from suffering, tears of sorrow for his bereaved family, tears of regret that the world would benefit no more by his talents, tears of loneliness for ourselves. We did not mourn because he was dead, for well we knew that to him death meant sweet, peaceful rest, and that to no man could rest be more welcome ; but we mourned for those he left behind, for our own loss, for the work which he would have done had he lived.

Colonel Monroe is dead. There may have been better men than he, there doubtless are abler men, but no man ever the better filled the positions in which he was placed. As a soldier he was brave, cool, devoted to duty, and rash only when rashness was a virtue; in his profession as civil engineer he embodied these qualities and joined to them judgment, talent, ability; as a man he was kind-hearted, generous, unassuming—a faithful husband, a kind father, a steadfast, true friend.

Having offered himself to serve our country, his keen sense of honor required him to fit himself to perform that service in the best manner he was able—to get out of himself for country's sake the best there was in him. How well he did this his army record shows, and I need not dwell upon it. Having fitted himself, and having confidence in himself as thus fitted, it was but second nature that in action he should be ready and able to take advantage of every opportunity and ever get the best out of his men and his guns. None did better than this. Of himself he never thought. His one object was to do his whole duty, to see that his men did their whole duty, and to make his guns tell upon the enemy. This is how he won the respect and praise of the general officers under whom he served, and was by them placed—where he belonged—among the best of artillerists and. bravest of officers. And yet, such was his make-up that he had no inordinate love of praise. It was pleasing to him, as to whom is it not, but he better loved the consciousness in his own heart of duty well done, of service well performed.

In his profession as civil engineer Colonel Monroe won an eminent position. He brought to his profession the same qualities which he took with him into the military service, enlarged and strengthened by experience and tempered by careful thought. There was the same study and labor to fit himself and to keep himself abreast of the highest; there was the same attention to details with the same ability to grapple with the whole problem; there was the same confidence in himself and the men under his direction; there was the same conscientiousness and thoroughness. He knew his profession and was sure of it. When he commenced a work, no matter how great its extent or its importance, he knew what the end would be, and no change which circumstances could render necessary in the details of his plans weakened his confidence in the final result, or prevented the completion of the work as he intended.

He was truly master of his profession. In him thought and action were so evenly balanced that the one neither hindered nor hastened the other. Action followed so closely upon thought that the two seemed to be one ; united they always were—always acting together—always in full accord with each other.

Whatever he set out to do, that he did, and well and thoroughly. He recognized no obstacles in the way of any duty in the field, or anything in his profession. In the mountains of the Catskills, in the snows of Dakotah, in the waters and mud of the every-varying bed of the Mississippi—everywhere, he compelled whatever stood in his way to submit to his will and skill. It was only when he was brought face to face with the ills of mortality that his will was overcome and he was obliged to surrender.

He was a good judge of human nature, and had a wonderful faculty of selecting the right men for his subordinates. Once he had confidence in a man he won that man's confidence. This gave him control of his men in the army and in civil life alike. He commanded their confidence by his confidence in them and in himself, and when he had once won their confidence and inspired their enthusiasm, as he always did, he could do anything man can do.

While Colonel Monroe could coolly look upon the havoc and devastation of battle, could calmly see his men—and men he loved—fall dead and wounded all around him, could send death and destruction among the enemy with the coolest calculation and skill and with the grim hope that every shot would tell, could look upon his own death as merely one of the incidents of war—he could also bring from the field of battle a letter found upon the body of a foeman, perhaps one whom his own fire had killed, the letter of a fond wife to her soldier husband, having in it a rude diagram of baby's hand drawn by the loving mother for the brave father to kiss, and could keep that letter and that diagram till his dying day, with feelings so tender that tears filled his eyes whenever he told the touching story.

Severe as were the tests of his courage in the army, Colonel Monroe faced, and nobly faced still more severe tests in civil life. He knew his own ability, but he could not bruit it abroad. He was neither courtier nor politician. He could not fawn

or beg for position. He was ever willing to be tried
on his merits, but could not ask a place by favor.
Consequently for years he stood well nigh still
while others went by him in the race, men of less
skill and less ability, and also of less modesty and
less self-esteem. He viewed this calmly and philo-
sophically, understanding it well, yet confident that
in time he would occupy the position in which he
belonged, and content to wait until that time came,
even though in the meantime he might be looked
upon by the many as a not successful man in his profession. Those were the times which brought out
his courage and manliness to their fullest extent and
in their highest sense. Out of business and need-
ing it sadly, he would not lower his manliness by
seeking business in what he considered an unworthy
manner, or degrade his profession by doing work
unworthy of his skill and ability. Calmly he passed
through those years, never losing confidence in himself, never losing faith that his time would come—
waiting patiently day after day, year after year, with
never a real hearty murmur, ever speaking of his situa-
tion and his prospects with a hope and confidence that

were tinted with the sublime. Those were the days when I learned to love and respect Colonel Monroe, when I learned what manner of man he was. His patient waiting was at last rewarded. He sprang into his proper place with a single bound, and with a single bound passed those who had passed him, and stood among the highest in his profession. From that time his works speak for him, and they are his best eulogists.

And yet, after all, what we loved and admired most in Colonel Monroe was his manhood, his sterling qualities, the steadfastness of his friendship, his manly adherence to what he thought was right, even when he stood alone—all the traits which go to make up a true man. We loved him for his worth as we respected him for his ability Of his domestic life it is not my province to speak. That is sacred to his family. They can tell the sweet, sad story as no others can, and to their bleeding hearts the story belongs.

Colonel Monroe is dead; but his noble example, his valiant services to our country, his grand work, will live till we are all long forgotten. As we looked

at his features for the last time we saw not the face
of agony which we had looked upon for months with
pity and with dread—not the face which told us how
a strong man may suffer without alleviation or hope,
and be brave through it all—not the face which had
been looking as calmly as the slow yet sure approach
of death by terrible, painful disease, as it had at the
quick, glorious, painless death in battle—but the
face we knew and loved so well when he was doing
his full share of the world's work and gloried in it,
the face of Col. J. Albert Monroe in sweet peace,
having on it a messenger from heaven, a suggestion
of the happy face with which he will give us a welcome greeting when we, too, shall have passed over
the pontoon which bridges the last river we all have
to cross.

www.ingramcontent.com/pod-product-compliance
Lightning Source LLC
Chambersburg PA
CBHW031815090426
42739CB00008B/1275